I0039239

Disorders of the Corpus Callosum and Confabulation: A Discovery Study

C. Wright, EDD

Sea Wright
PUBLISHING

Copyright © 2017 Cheryl Wright

All rights reserved.

ISBN: 1-947702-01-7
ISBN-13: 978-1-947702-01-1

DEDICATION

To Egbert B. Gebstadter, my tulpa, for keeping me on track.

CONTENTS

ACKNOWLEDGMENTS

I am continually amazed by the community of people associated with Disorders of the Corpus Callosum. Thank you for your participation and I hope this body of research can contribute in a positive way.

1 CONFABULATION

The connectivity of the human brain endows it with complexity. The corpus callosum, the largest connective structure in the brain, is often referred to as the bridge between the brain's hemispheres. In simple terms, it is the information superhighway between the left and right hemispheres. It is estimated that 1 in 3,000 people are born with a disorder of the corpus callosum. Disorders of the Corpus Callosum (DCC) is an encompassing definition that includes thinning of the corpus callosum, malformation, partial absence, acquired damage to the corpus callosum, as well as a complete absence of the corpus callosum connective structure. A variety of developmental, physical, behavioral, cognitive, and language difficulties are associated with DCC. Confabulation, or the telling of misinformation without deceitful intent or knowledge, is a symptom that is associated with DCC that has yet to be quantified.

Confabulation is such an enigmatic quality that the very definition has proven to be a difficult and controversial topic. Although, confabulation can assume many forms, traditionally the definition includes (1) false (2) reports (3) about memories. Confabulation can include unintentionally incongruous statements or verbalization about the past, present, or future. The definition of confabulation can alternately include or exclude false memories and delusions.

People confabulate for a variety of reasons. Physical and mental age as well as culture are considerations. An experience with Santa Claus, the Tooth Fairy or ghosts could be considered confabulations. Propaganda or indoctrination could have crossover implications. Physical and mental health may be a factor. Does the person have PTSD, schizophrenia, alcohol dependency, or other physical consideration? Situational health should be considered. Has the person been exposed to poisons, medications, or other mind altering substances? Care should be given to situational experience. Was there something about the situation that caused a visual or other sensory misinterpretation such as an echo, reflection of light, or swamp gas? Is the person color deficient? Adding to the difficulty, some people are aware of their confabulation and some are not.

Confabulation has been associated with many diseases and injuries. It was first associated with Korsakoff patients and cognitively impaired chronic alcoholics. It has since been associated with lesions, psychiatric disorders, post-traumatic stress disorder, traumatic brain injury, and medications. Confabulation, more recently, is associated with a variety of brain differences. Data from numerous studies suggested organic brain differences and injury is an agency in confabulation. The prevalence of confabulation within the community of people with DCC had yet to be quantified.

2 CLASSIFICATION AND

RATAING SCALES FOR CONFABULATION

Historically the authors of research on confabulation fit their categories of different types of confabulation to their observations. Researchers have classified confabulation under the following subgroups: memory confabulations, confabulations about intentions and actions, perceptual confabulations, and confabulations about emotions. Assessments for confabulation often break the categories into: spontaneous confabulation, provoked confabulation, and memory and orientation. At present the development of instruments to study confabulation, as well as standard definitions are in evolution.

Assessments of confabulation can be implemented in two ways

1) A real-time test. To test if the person is confabulating at the moment; assess the general knowledge of personal semantics, memory, orientation in time and place, and general semantic memory of the participants.

2) Observations, questionnaires, or interviews to ask about a history of confabulation.

Confabulation measures were explored to find a suitable test to determine the prevalence of confabulation within the community of people with DCC in this discovery investigation. Previous measures of confabulation were reviewed for appropriateness including Dalla Barba's confabulations measures, the Gudjonsson Suggestibility Scales (GSS), the Bonn Test of Statement Suggestibility (BTSS), the Sacramento Assessment of Confabulation (SAC), and the Nijmegen-Venray Confabulation List (NVCL-20). Strengths and limitations of each test were explored.

Dalla Barba measured confabulation quantitatively. He required participants to answer a variety of questions, which required episodic memory and long-term memory (including memory for famous people and events). Unfortunately, Dalla Barba's questions were idiosyncratic to French—e.g., French athletes, politicians, and battles.

The Gudjonsson Suggestibility Scales (GSS) and the Bonn Test of Statement Suggestibility (BTSS) are the most used tools for assessing interrogative suggestibility. Apart from minor differences, the two tests investigate the same dimensions. These are used to measure suggestibility and could be used to test provoked confabulations.

The Sacramento Assessment of Confabulation (SAC) was developed to add precision to the description of confabulation and establish whether confabulation can be considered on a continuum. The instrument also was developed as a measure to determine whether individuals who confabulate, with intervention, have a potential for recovery. An additional subtest valued one's willingness to "not know". The SAC was used to assess the general knowledge of personal semantics, memory, orientation in time and place, and general semantic memory of the participants. The SAC, like Dalla Barba's confabulation measures, included questions that are date sensitive and would need to be assessed before using with a recent population.

The Nijmegen-Venray Confabulation List (NVCL-20) is an observation scale to measure spontaneous confabulation. The items on this scale cover spontaneous confabulation, provoked confabulation, and memory and orientation (Rensen et al., 2015). The researchers noted:

> The NVCL-20 has been validated in Korsakoff patients and cognitively impaired chronic alcoholics. Their ratings were related to the Dalla Barba Confabulation Battery (DBCB), Provoked Confabulation Test (PCT), and standard neuropsychological tests. The categories of the NVCL-20 have "good" to "excellent" internal consistency and inter-rater agreement. Administration is reliable, valid and feasible in clinical practice, making it a useful addition to existing confabulating measures. (Rensen et al., 2015, p. 804)

After careful consideration a modified version of the NVCL-20 was deemed the most appropriate test for this discovery investigation.

3 THE SURVEY

The research began with exploration and design of a survey that would be appropriate for exploring confabulation in the DCC population. The Trait Study in Persons with Disorders of the Corpus Callosum (DCC) questionnaire was modeled closely after The Nijmegen-Venray Confabulation List (NVCL-20), which is a confabulation test with scale items that cover spontaneous confabulation, provoked confabulation, and memory and orientation. It was developed to explore confabulation and used with Korsakoff patients and cognitively impaired chronic alcoholics. The closely related Trait Study in Persons with Disorders of the Corpus Callosum (DCC) questionnaire explores incidences of confabulation in persons with disorders of the corpus callosum.

The survey was sent out to individuals with DCC and community who interact with individuals with DCC via a topical listserve group facilitated by the University of Maine, as well as several special interest groups on social media that serve this community. This survey asked for demographical information such as age of the person with DCC, and whether they were self-reporting or reporting on someone they know with a DCC. It was important to also survey a sample that does and does not have familiarity and experience with confabulation. To prevent participation bias, the survey introduction asked the participants if they were willing to participate in a survey on characteristic traits in people with DCC and not just confabulation. This was done in order not to prejudice the type of participants that are willing to answer the survey. There may be an over-reporting bias for people that have had experience with confabulation to answer a survey on confabulation whereas a better sample of the population could be gleaned from a survey entitled Trait Study of People with Disorders of the Corpus Callosum.

The content validity of the Trait Study of People with Disorders of the Corpus Callosum questionnaire was estimated through the use of a Content Validity Index (CVI) on which experts in the area of confabulation and DCC rated the content of the survey instrument for relevance, giving the instrument validity. The CVI involved highly qualified raters to judge each of the 22 questions on the DCC questionnaire as to the relevance to each in the understanding of confabulation in persons with a disorder of the corpus callosum. The raters consisted of two Ph.D. holders who have written on confabulation, an M.D. who is an expert on Disorders of the Corpus Callosum, two registered nurses with experience with people with DCC and confabulations, a Juris Doctor familiar with confabulation, a Doctor of Education familiar with DCC and confabulation, and an author on TBI and confabulation with a Master's of Physical Therapy. Each of the 22 questions was scored on a 1-4 scale: 1 = Not Relevant, 2 = Somewhat Relevant, 3 = Quite Relevant, 4 = Highly Relevant. Raters provided a single rating for each question. The CVI yielded overall Kappa value for the instrument of 1.00, a perfect rating. This showed strong conceptualizations of constructs, good items, and judiciously selected experts. This rating indicated the raters were in very high agreement that the individual questions were highly relevant to the concept of confabulation.

The population targeted was exclusively adult individuals. Both individuals with a corpus callosum disorder, for self-reporting, and the community that interacts with children and adults with corpus callosum disorders, for second-person accounts and perceptions were invited to participate. All participants who answered the survey were asked to certify as being 18 years or older. The subject, the person about whom the survey taker is talking, could have been under 18. For example, a father may have given information regarding his experiences with a child who has DCC. The sample included individuals with DCC and members of the population reporting on others with DCC.

This study is exploring incidences of confabulation in persons with Disorders of the Corpus Callosum (DCC). Please answer this questionnaire about **one** person.

Confabulation can be defined as communicating information that is untrue while perceiving that i is true.

There are 30 questions. If at any time you would like to stop this survey, you can.

Trait Study in Persons with Disorders of the Corpus Callosum (DCC)

Q1.

INFORMED CONSENT DOCUMENT
Project Title: Survey of Reported Rates of Confabulation in Persons with Disorders of the Corpus Callosum
Investigator: Cheryl L. Wright,
You are being asked to participate in a project conducted through Western Kentucky University. The University requires that you give your signed agreement to participate in this project.
You must be 18 years old or older to participate in this research study.

1. Nature and Purpose of the Project:
The corpus callosum is the largest bundle of nerve fibers in the brain. It forms the connections between the right and left hemispheres of the brain. When someone has a condition where the corpus callosum did not develop in a typical manner they are said to have a disorder of the corpus callosum.
Confabulation, communicating information that is untrue while perceiving that it is true, is among the list of possible challenges for people with Disorders of the Corpus Callosum (DCC). People with DCC may have subtle differences in the way they perceive and react. The prevalence and significance of confabulation within the community of people with DCC has yet to be fully explored. This research attempts to begin data collection on the topic.
2. Explanation of Procedures:
Participants are asked to complete the 15 minute survey. A mixed group of people with a DCC, friends, family, and professionals will be encouraged to participate.
3. **Discomfort and Risks:**
There are no known risks to the subjects.
4. Benefits:
The prevalence and significance of confabulation within the community of people with DCC has yet to be fully explored. The goal of this research is to help define this possible challenge to the DCC community.

This survey has 30 questions and should take about 15 minutes to complete.

Q2. I am 18 years old or older.

○ Yes

○ No. Thank you for your time. Please end this survey.

Q3. **Please only answer this survey about one person.**
How do you know the person with a Disorder of the Corpus Callosum (DCC)? (Pick as many as apply.)

☐ Self. (I have a Disorder of the Corpus Callosum, and am answering this survey about myself.)

☐ Family Member. (The person with the Disorder of the Corpus Callosum is someone in my family.)

☐ Friend.

☐ Teacher. (I am a teacher for someone with a Disorder of the Corpus Callosum.)

☐ Medical Professional.

○ Other.

_____

Q4. Age of person with the Disorder of the Corpus Callosum.

○ Under 14

○ 14-17 years old

○ 18-20 years old

○ 21-25 years old

○ 26-30 years old

○ 31-35 years old

○ 36-40 years old

○ 41-45 years old

○ 46+

○ Unknown. Please provide approximate age

_____

Q5.
Confabulation can be defined as communicating information that is untrue while perceiving that it is true.
Does the person with the Disorder of the Corpus Callosum (DCC) confabulate spontaneously (on their own without prompting)?

○ Never

○ Rarely

○ Sometimes

○ Often

○ (almost) Always

Q6. Does (s)he spontaneously tell stories that are incorrect with respect to time and/or place?

○ Never

○ Rarely

○ Sometimes

○ Often

○ (almost) Always

Q7. How often does the person with DCC spontaneously confabulate?

○ Rarely to never

○ A few times a week

○ Almost every day

○

Several times a day

○ This happens almost continuously

Q8.
Is the content of the confabulations realistic? Would someone who does not know the person with DCC believe him/her? (An example of realistic, the person wants to go out to work. Not realistic, the person tells you that (s)he has a meeting with the Queen?)

○ The stories are realistic (if the context is not being taken into account)

○ Some elements of the story do not seem to be plausible

○ An outsider would have doubts about the truth of the story (meeting a famous person, being very rich)

○ It is obvious that some elements of the story cannot be true

○ The stories are very hard to believe

Q9. Does the person with DCC tell you or others that (s)he has an appointment with others (family, doctor) when this is not the case?

○ Never

○ Rarely

○ Sometimes

○ Often

○ (almost) Always

Q10. Does the person with DCC tell you or others that (s)he had visitors who in fact never visited him/her?

○ Never

○ Rarely

○ Sometimes

○ Often

○ (almost) Always

Q11.
Does the person with DCC believe to be somewhere else other than where (s)he actually is?

○ Never

○ Rarely

○ Sometimes

○ Often

○ (almost) Always

Q12.
Are the confabulations coherent stories, or are they difficult to follow and highly associative?

○ The stories are coherent and easy to follow

○ The stories are usually easy to follow, but some details are incorrect

○ The gist of the stories is clear, but details are incorrect and the patient frequently changes the subject

○ The stories are difficult to follow, the person often changes the subject

○ the person rambles and tells stories that are difficult to follow, swerves off topic

Q13.
Can the person be corrected when telling these stories?

○ Yes, the person immediately assumes that (s)he is incorrect

○ Yes, it only takes a little persuasion to convince the person that (s)he is mistaken

○ Sometimes, the person occasionally sticks to his/her conviction

○ Usually not, only confronting him/her with the incorrectness of a story results in

○ reconsideration (e.g., an outside temperature of 25°C when the patient states that it is winter)

○ Usually not, only confronting him/her with the incorrectness of a story results in reconsideration (e.g., an outside temperature of 80°F when the person states that it is winter)

○ No, the person cannot be convinced of the reality and reacts negatively on efforts to do so

Q14.
Does the person recognizes acquaintances correctly?

○ Yes, always

○ Often

○ Sometimes

○ Rarely

○ No, never

Q15.
Does the person show incorrect familiarity ('recognize' strangers, or mistake people for someone else)?

○ Never

○ Rarely

○ Sometimes

○ Often

○ (almost) Always

Q16.
Does the person see or hear things that are not present?

○ Never

○ Rarely

11

○ Sometimes

○ Often

○ (almost) Always

Q17.
When the person is being asked about what (s)he is presently doing, does (s)he respond correctly?

○ Yes, always: the person responds correctly to where (s)he is and why

○ Often

○ Sometimes

○ Rarely

○ No, never: the person does not know where (s)he is and why

Q18.
When the person is being asked what (s)he did yesterday, does (s)he answer correctly?

○ Yes, always

○ Often

○ Sometimes

○ Rarely

○ No, never

Q19.
When the person is being asked about plans for the day or the next weekend, does the person answer correctly?

○ Yes, always

○ Often

○ Sometimes

○ Rarely

○ No, never

Q20.
When the person is being asked about something (s)he does not remember anymore, (s)he admit this?

○ Yes, always

○ Often

○ Sometimes

○ Rarely

○ No, never

Q21.
Does the person act upon his/her confabulations? Does (s)he for example walk to the door to wait for somebody

or does (s)he get up during a conversation to take care of the dog?

- Never
- Rarely
- Sometimes
- Often
- (almost) Always

Q22
How often does the person act or want to act upon the confabulations?

- Rarely to never
- A few times a week
- Almost daily
- Several times per day
- This happens almost continuously

Q23.
Is the person well oriented to place?

- Yes, the person can correctly name the name and location of where (s)he is
- Fairly, the person is usually able to correctly tell where (s)he is
- So-so, the person cannot always correctly provide the location name and place
- Poorly, the person cannot correctly tell where (s)he is and often thinks (s)he is somewhere else
- Very poorly, the person is convinced to be somewhere else

Q24
Is the person well oriented to calendar dates?

- Yes, the person can correctly name the date and year
- Fairly, the person is sometimes one day wrong
- So-so, the person can tell the month and year but not the date
- Poorly, the person can tell which season it is, but not the date of month
- Very poorly, the person cannot name the date and is often several months or years off

Q25. Is the person well oriented to time?

- Yes, the person can correctly tell and keep time
- Fairly, the person can read a clock but can not predict the time
- So-so, the person can understand appointment times but can not keep track of the passage of time
- Poorly, the person does not understand appointment times but understands the need to be on time
- Very poorly, the person does not have a concept of time

Q26.
Is the person capable of remembering things, such as names of other people or appointments?

○ Yes, (s)he can do this with out problems

○ Fairly, it is sometimes necessary to repeat things

○ So-so, information must be presented several times

○ Poorly, only names of people which (s)he is in frequent contact will be remembered

○ Very Poorly the person does not see to profit from repetition and names of other people are not remembered

Q27. Is the person with DCC

○ Male

○ Female

○ Other

Q28. Please provide your email address (Used to prevent duplication only. Your information will not be shared.)

[   ]

Q29. OPTIONAL QUESTION
Further Comments

[   ]

Q30. OPTIONAL QUESTION
The person with the Disorder of the Corpus Callosum Disorder: (You may choose more than one.)

☐ (ACC) Agenesis of the corpus callosum: All or a portion of the corpus callosum is absent; this includes both complete and partial ACC

☐ (AgCC) Agenesis of the corpus callosum: All or a portion of the corpus callosum is absent. This acronym has appeared more recently in some research literature.

☐ (c-ACC) Complete agenesis of the corpus callosum: The corpus callosum is completely absent.

☐ (p-ACC) Partial agenesis of the corpus callosum: A portion of the corpus callosum is absent; most often it is the posterior (back) portion that is missing.

☐ Hypogenesis of the corpus callosum: Another term sometimes used to describe partial ACC.

☐ Hypoplasia of the corpus callosum: The corpus callosum is present, but is abnormally thin.

☐ Dysgenesis of the corpus callosum: The corpus callosum is present but is malformed in some way; this includes p-ACC and Hypoplasia.

☐ Unknown or Other
[   ]

Q31. OPTIONAL QUESTION
Does the person with DCC have other health or behavior concerns? Please list.

4 RESULTS

There were a total of 170 respondents to the survey, with 139 surveys mostly completed. All participants were pulled from social media groups and a conference directly involved with people with DCC. All respondents were over the age of 18. As people with DCC may have associated anosognosia, or a deficit in self- awareness, this study included the perceptions of the individuals with DCC as well as the community that interacts with them. Data came from family, friends, medical professionals, educational professionals, and other individuals who have associations with the population with DCC. Respondents with DCC could self-report if 18 or older; the associated group could report on an individual under the age of 18. This discovery study examined frequency and types of confabulation as a means to understand whether confabulation is a concern for those with DCC.

Q2 - I am 18 years old or older.

99%
Yes

■ Yes ■ No. Thank you for your time. Please end this survey.

There were 155 respondents; 154 = yes, 1 = no. The no respondent was disqualified.

Q3 - Please only answer this survey about one person. How do you know the person with a Disorder of the Corpus Callosum (DCC)? (Pick as many as apply.)

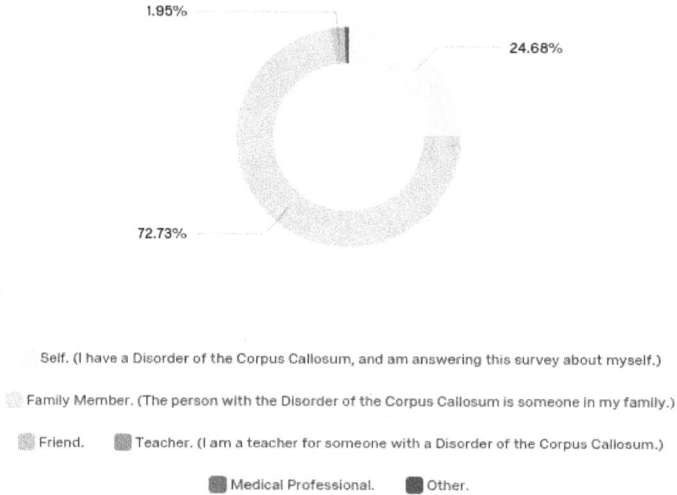

1.95%

24.68%

72.73%

Self. (I have a Disorder of the Corpus Callosum, and am answering this survey about myself.)

Family Member. (The person with the Disorder of the Corpus Callosum is someone in my family.)

Friend.   Teacher. (I am a teacher for someone with a Disorder of the Corpus Callosum.)

Medical Professional.   Other.

#	Answer	%	Count
1	Self. (I have a Disorder of the Corpus Callosum, and am answering this survey about myself.)	24.68%	38
2	Family Member. (The person with the Disorder of the Corpus Callosum is someone in my family.)	72.73%	112
3	Friend.	1.95%	3
4	Teacher. (I am a teacher for someone with a Disorder of the Corpus Callosum.)	0.00%	0
5	Medical Professional.	0.00%	0
6	Other.	0.65%	1
	Total	100%	154

Q4 - Age of person with the Disorder of the Corpus Callosum.

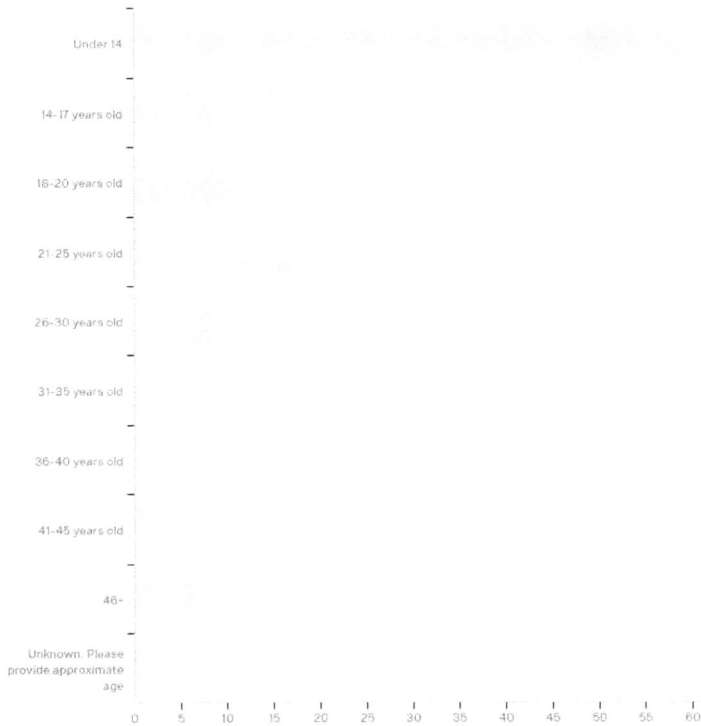

#	Answer	%	Count
1	Under 14	38.82%	59
2	14-17 years old	10.53%	16
3	18-20 years old	9.21%	14
4	21-25 years old	13.16%	20
5	26-30 years old	9.21%	14
6	31-35 years old	4.61%	7
7	36-40 years old	6.58%	10
8	41-45 years old	2.63%	4
9	46+	4.61%	7
10	Unknown. Please provide approximate age	0.66%	1
	Total	100%	152

Q5 - Confabulation can be defined as communicating information that is untrue while perceiving that it is true. Does the person with the Disorder of the Corpus Callosum (DCC) confabulate spontaneously (on their own without prompting)?

#	Answer	%	Count
1	Never	29.50%	41
2	Rarely	22.30%	31
3	Sometimes	32.37%	45
4	Often	12.23%	17
5	(almost) Always	3.60%	5
	Total	100%	139

Q6 - Does (s)he spontaneously tell stories that are incorrect with respect to time and/or place?

#	Answer	%	Count
1	Never	27.13%	35
2	Rarely	19.38%	25
3	Sometimes	33.33%	43
4	Often	15.50%	20
5	(almost) Always	4.65%	6
	Total	100%	129

Q7 - How often does the person with DCC spontaneously confabulate?

#	Answer	%	Count
1	Rarely to never	52.38%	66
2	A few times a week	31.75%	40
3	Almost every day	9.52%	12
4	Several times a day	4.76%	6
5	This happens almost continuously	1.59%	2
	Total	100%	126

Q8 - Is the content of the confabulations realistic? Would someone who does not know the person with DCC believe him/her? (An example of realistic, the person wants to go out to work. Not realistic, the person tells you that (s)he has a meeting with the Queen?)

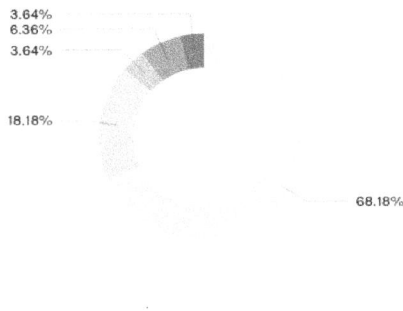

3.64%
6.36%
3.64%

18.18%

68.18%

The stories are realistic (if the context is not being taken into account)

Some elements of the story do not seem to be plausible

An outsider would have doubts about the truth of the story (meeting a famous person, being very rich)

It is obvious that some elements of the story cannot be true   The stories are very hard to believe

#	Answer	%	Count
1	The stories are realistic (if the context is not being taken into account)	68.18%	75
2	Some elements of the story do not seem to be plausible	18.18%	20
3	An outsider would have doubts about the truth of the story (meeting a famous person, being very rich)	3.64%	4
4	It is obvious that some elements of the story cannot be true	6.36%	7
5	The stories are very hard to believe	3.64%	4
	Total	100%	110

Q9 - Does the person with DCC tell you or others that (s)he has an appointment with others (family, doctor) when this is not the case?

#	Answer	%	Count
1	Never	69.72%	76
2	Rarely	15.60%	17
3	Sometimes	10.09%	11
4	Often	4.59%	5
5	(almost) Always	0.00%	0
	Total	100%	109

Q10 - Does the person with DCC tell you or others that (s)he had visitors who in fact never visited him/her?

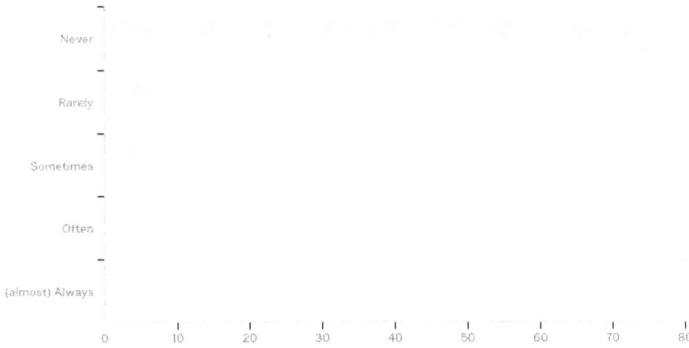

#	Answer	%	Count
1	Never	71.96%	77
2	Rarely	11.21%	12
3	Sometimes	11.21%	12
4	Often	4.67%	5
5	(almost) Always	0.93%	1
	Total	100%	107

Q11 - Does the person with DCC believe to be somewhere else other than where (s)he actually is?

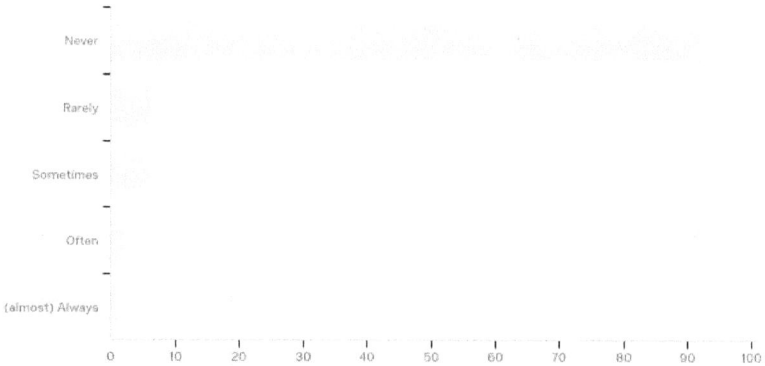

#	Answer	%	Count
1	Never	85.98%	92
2	Rarely	5.61%	6
3	Sometimes	5.61%	6
4	Often	1.87%	2
5	(almost) Always	0.93%	1
	Total	100%	107

Q12 - Are the confabulations coherent stories, or are they difficult to follow and highly associative?

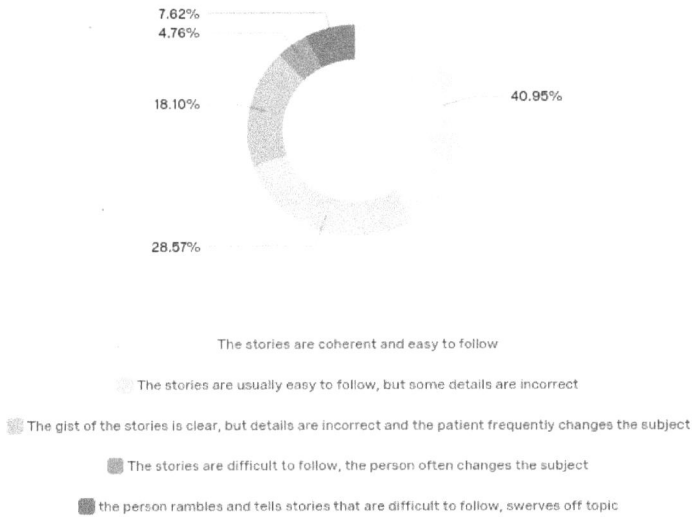

7.62%
4.76%

18.10%

40.95%

28.57%

The stories are coherent and easy to follow

The stories are usually easy to follow, but some details are incorrect

The gist of the stories is clear, but details are incorrect and the patient frequently changes the subject

The stories are difficult to follow, the person often changes the subject

the person rambles and tells stories that are difficult to follow, swerves off topic

#	Answer	%	Count
1	The stories are coherent and easy to follow	40.95%	43
2	The stories are usually easy to follow, but some details are incorrect	28.57%	30
3	The gist of the stories is clear, but details are incorrect and the patient frequently changes the subject	18.10%	19
4	The stories are difficult to follow, the person often changes the subject	4.76%	5
5	the person rambles and tells stories that are difficult to follow, swerves off topic	7.62%	8
	Total	100%	105

Q13 - Can the person be corrected when telling these stories?

17.82% 18.81%

5.94%

3.96%

20.79% 32.67%

Yes, the person immediately assumes that (s)he is incorrect

Yes, it only takes a little persuasion to convince the person that (s)he is mistaken

Sometimes, the person occasionally sticks to his/her conviction

Usually not, only confronting him/her with the incorrectness of a story results in

reconsideration (e.g., an outside temperature of 25°C when the patient states that it is winter)

Usually not, only confronting him/her with the incorrectness of a story results in reconsideration (e.g., an

outside temperature of 80°F when the person states that it is winter)

No, the person cannot be convinced of the reality and reacts negatively on efforts to do so

#	Answer	%	Count
1	Yes, the person immediately assumes that (s)he is incorrect	18.81%	19
2	Yes, it only takes a little persuasion to convince the person that (s)he is mistaken	32.67%	33
3	Sometimes, the person occasionally sticks to his/her conviction	20.79%	21
4	Usually not, only confronting him/her with the incorrectness of a story results in	3.96%	4
5	reconsideration (e.g., an outside temperature of 25°C when the patient states that it is winter)	0.00%	0
6	Usually not, only confronting him/her with the incorrectness of a story results in reconsideration (e.g., an outside temperature of 80°F when the person states that it is winter)	5.94%	6
7	No, the person cannot be convinced of the reality and reacts negatively on efforts to do so	17.82%	18

| Total | 100% | 101 |

Q14 - Does the person recognizes acquaintances correctly?

#	Answer	%	Count
1	Yes, always	64.00%	64
2	Often	20.00%	20
3	Sometimes	12.00%	12
4	Rarely	4.00%	4
5	No, never	0.00%	0
	Total	100%	100

Q15 - Does the person show incorrect familiarity ('recognize' strangers, or mistake people for someone else)?

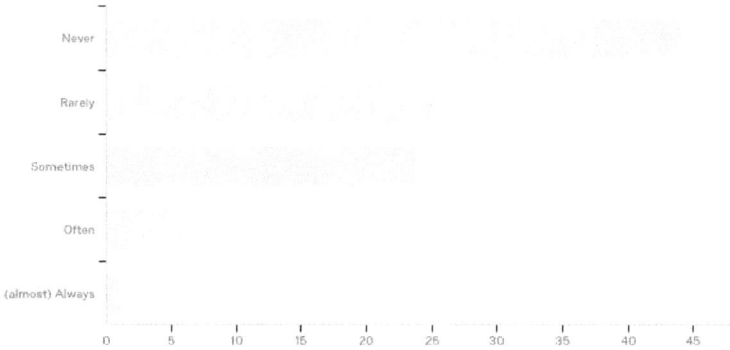

#	Answer	%	Count
1	Never	44.00%	44
2	Rarely	25.00%	25
3	Sometimes	24.00%	24
4	Often	6.00%	6
5	(almost) Always	1.00%	1
	Total	100%	100

Q16 - Does the person see or hear things that are not present?

#	Answer	%	Count
1	Never	63.00%	63
2	Rarely	23.00%	23
3	Sometimes	10.00%	10
4	Often	3.00%	3
5	(almost) Always	1.00%	1
	Total	100%	100

Q17 - When the person is being asked about what (s)he is presently doing, does (s)he respond correctly?

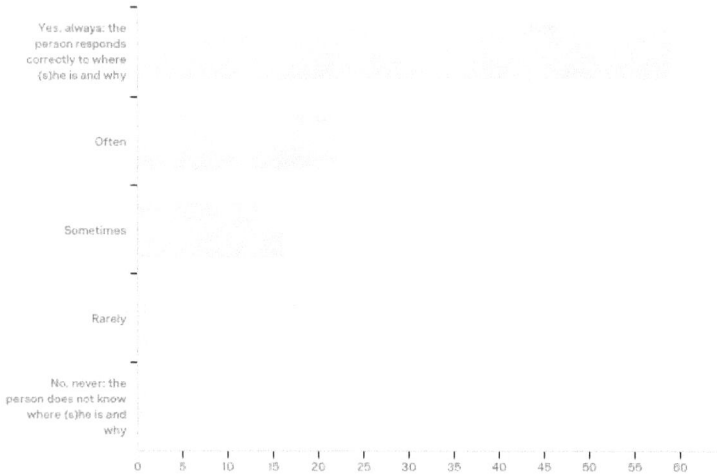

#	Answer	%	Count
1	Yes, always: the person responds correctly to where (s)he is and why	59.60%	59
2	Often	22.22%	22
3	Sometimes	16.16%	16
4	Rarely	1.01%	1
5	No, never: the person does not know where (s)he is and why	1.01%	1
	Total	100%	99

Q18 - When the person is being asked what (s)he did yesterday, does (s)he answer correctly?

#	Answer	%	Count
1	Yes, always	36.36%	36
2	Often	29.29%	29
3	Sometimes	21.21%	21
4	Rarely	11.11%	11
5	No, never	2.02%	2
	Total	100%	99

Q19 - When the person is being asked about plans for the day or the next weekend, does the person answer correctly?

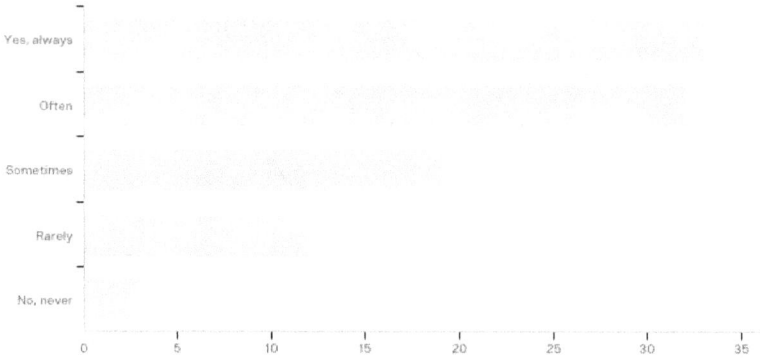

#	Answer	%	Count
1	Yes, always	33.33%	33
2	Often	32.32%	32
3	Sometimes	19.19%	19
4	Rarely	12.12%	12
5	No, never	3.03%	3
	Total	100%	99

Q20 - When the person is being asked about something (s)he does not remember anymore, (s)he admit this?

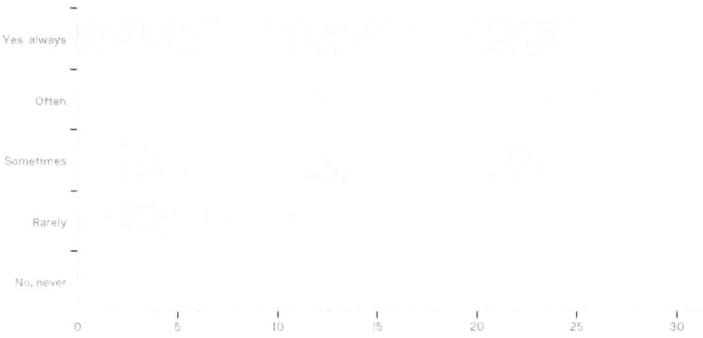

Yes, always						
Often						
Sometimes						
Rarely						
No, never						
0	5	10	15	20	25	30

#	Answer	%	Count
1	Yes, always	25.25%	25
2	Often	27.27%	27
3	Sometimes	29.29%	29
4	Rarely	11.11%	11
5	No, never	7.07%	7
	Total	100%	99

33

Q21 - Does the person act upon his/her confabulations? Does (s)he for example walk to the door to wait for somebody or does (s)he get up during a conversation to take care of the dog?

#	Answer	%	Count
1	Never	58.16%	57
2	Rarely	17.35%	17
3	Sometimes	15.31%	15
4	Often	7.14%	7
5	(almost) Always	2.04%	2
	Total	100%	98

Q22 - How often does the person act or want to act upon the confabulations?

#	Answer	%	Count
1	Rarely to never	73.47%	72
2	A few times a week	18.37%	18
3	Almost daily	5.10%	5
4	Several times per day	2.04%	2
5	This happens almost continuously	1.02%	1
	Total	100%	98

Q23 - Is the person well oriented to place?

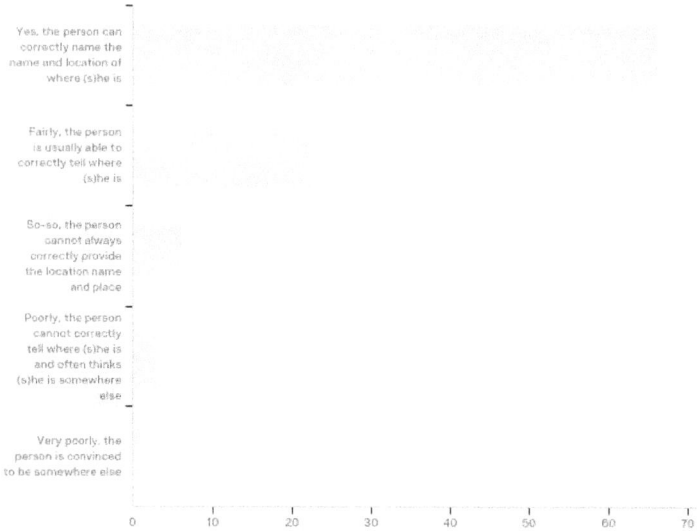

#	Answer	%	Count
1	Yes, the person can correctly name the name and location of where (s)he is	67.35%	66
2	Fairly, the person is usually able to correctly tell where (s)he is	22.45%	22
3	So-so, the person cannot always correctly provide the location name and place	6.12%	6
4	Poorly, the person cannot correctly tell where (s)he is and often thinks (s)he is somewhere else	3.06%	3
5	Very poorly, the person is convinced to be somewhere else	1.02%	1
	Total	100%	98

Q24 - Is the person well oriented to calendar dates?

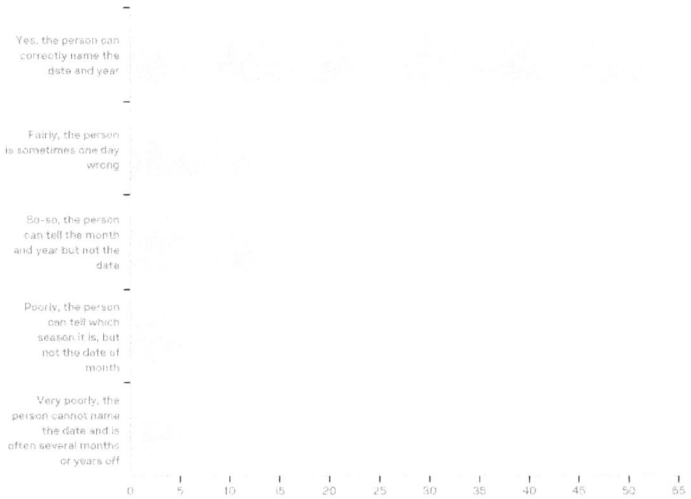

#	Answer	%	Count
1	Yes, the person can correctly name the date and year	53.61%	52
2	Fairly, the person is sometimes one day wrong	19.59%	19
3	So-so, the person can tell the month and year but not the date	14.43%	14
4	Poorly, the person can tell which season it is, but not the date of month	5.15%	5
5	Very poorly, the person cannot name the date and is often several months or years off	7.22%	7
	Total	100%	97

Q25 - Is the person well oriented to time?

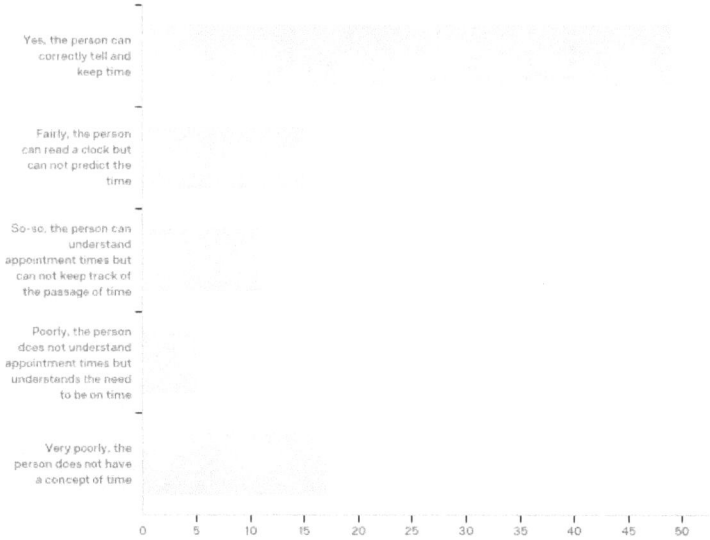

#	Answer	%	Count
1	Yes, the person can correctly tell and keep time	50.52%	49
2	Fairly, the person can read a clock but can not predict the time	15.46%	15
3	So-so, the person can understand appointment times but can not keep track of the passage of time	11.34%	11
4	Poorly, the person does not understand appointment times but understands the need to be on time	5.15%	5
5	Very poorly, the person does not have a concept of time	17.53%	17
	Total	100%	97

Q26 - Is the person capable of remembering things, such as names of other people or appointments?

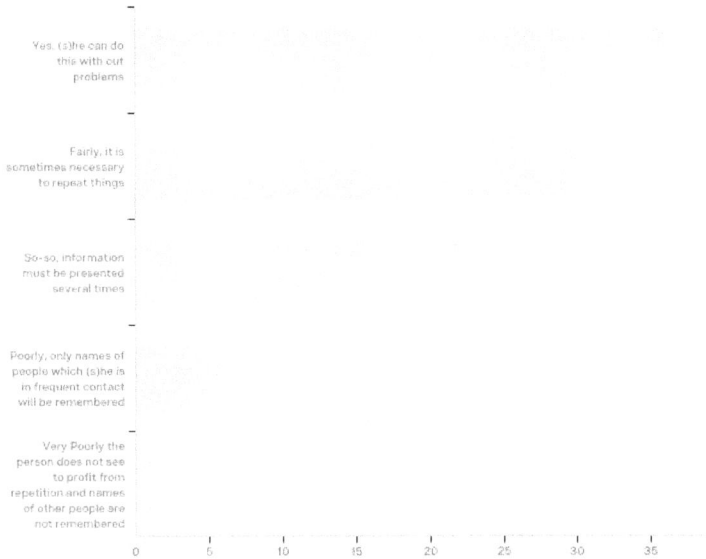

#	Answer	%	Count
1	Yes, (s)he can do this with out problems	37.11%	36
2	Fairly, it is sometimes necessary to repeat things	30.93%	30
3	So-so, information must be presented several times	22.68%	22
4	Poorly, only names of people which (s)he is in frequent contact will be remembered	6.19%	6
5	Very Poorly the person does not see to profit from repetition and names of other people are not remembered	3.09%	3
	Total	100%	97

Q27 - Is the person with DCC

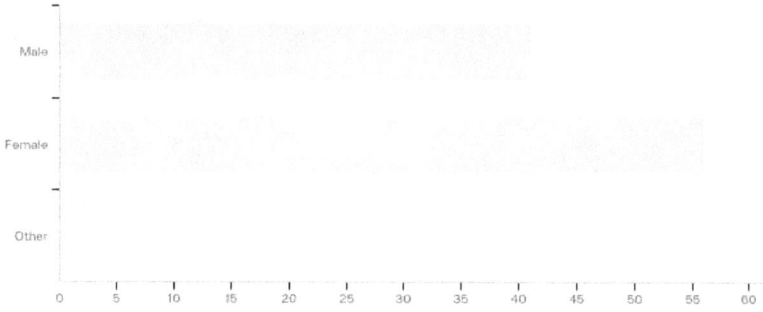

#	Answer	%	Count
1	Male	42.27%	41
2	Female	57.73%	56
3	Other	0.00%	0
	Total	100%	97

Q29 - OPTIONAL QUESTION Further Comments

OPTIONAL QUESTION Further Comments

My son often distorts the truth because he fears getting in trouble (pretends he doesn't know something to avoid consequences). Other times he lies to avoid doing work. When I confront him with evidence after catching him in a lie, he often responds with "Are you sure?" I do think he loses track of distinguishing between reality and delirium.

My son is 6.

Nope.

Since his Dad & I divorced, and he has residential custody of him, he is influenced by my ex's Narcisstic behavior, so I'm insure whether the confabulation is based on influence, misdirected guilt or allegiance. I filled this out to the best of my knowledge given all I know of my son's development.

This questionnaire makes people with DCC seem delusional or liars.it's hard to answer some of these questions when most of them don't pertain to our daughter .

I thought this was only happening with my child, interesting to note that it likely happens with many who have DCC.

Interesting. She is XXXXX and seems pretty typical in this regard when compared to other kids. Her XXXXX, however, really struggles with confabulation. The family thinks he has autism, though no one will confront him to get a diagnosis because of his age. He has had an MRI, so we know he doesn't have DCC.

Mostly unattainable aspirations. When he is

President, or a pro wrestler, or wins an Olympic medal, cures diabetes or buys the airline that cancelled our flight.

confabulation occurred mostly as a child and teen and usually in relation to having done something wrong and unable to admit to it.

Sure

Her confab relate to her skill levels and social prowess. She overestimates and denies need for any assistance. She confabulated much more as a youth but very little as a 19 year old.

i have partial acc

Make less confusing questions I'm also dyslexic do make the question easier for dyslexic people because I don't know what the word confabulation means

My son is 2X years of age, graduated at age of 2X with special needs diploma and we are still fighting for SSDI,, he has EXTREME social anxiety but you could never tell by looking at him that he had any issues. They label him as high functioning which he is and I know that I am blessed because he is able, but with reminding to do everything and constant redirection. His bathing etc is also an issue . Thanks for the questions kinda made me not feel so alone.

I wonder if there is a difference between confabulation and not being able to remember or predict. The question that struck the biggest chord for me was the understanding appointment times but not the passage of time. Most of my son's issues are interpretation of the facts, not that he is trying to make it different but he can't see the gray scales. It is black and white.

I think the problem is more related to confusion than "lying". He doesn't remember faces/names, and doesn't have a good sense of how long things take to do, or directions. Perhaps your next survey could address that as an option.

additional questions re what situations are iikely to result in conflabulations seem to be needed

I would say that this does not relate to my daughter. Although, she may take things out of context and over react. Such as; us calling her honey, she doesn't like it because she doesn't want to be associated with a sticky mess that comes from bees. Or, another instance, she took a sex respect class in middle school and they talked about inappropriate touching, she didn't want to be hugged by us and thought it was inappropriate touching. She still has issues with hugging or showing affection with people even her own family members.

Person is 10 years of age

One interesting observation is when my family member with ACC answers questions about a situation, event, or conversation, she will give one answer in the moment, but then when asked the same question later that day or a day or two thereafter, she will have a different answer.

no comment. good continuation

2 of your questions need a "does not apply" option...
When reporting things that happened at school did the incident happen to them or someone else. Could even apply to work.

I am not someone who confabulates. However, I answered a question to how I tell stories to others as 'rambling' and moving off topic. Similar to someone who had ADHD.

Some of these questions did not pertain to my family member because he is non verbal. There should have been a N/A response.

Thank you

The biggest issue is the inability to correctly interpret some situations or encounters, leading to different perceptions of things that happened or what was said.

She doesn't make up stories. I would phrase it more as her misinterpreting social issues. For example, her XXXXX teacher played XXXXXX, by XXXXXX. Being somewhat unfamiliar with the song, I downloaded it so that we could listen to it at home and get familiar with it. She has now decided that I love all things XXXXX and am obsessed with them. This results in my having to have a very bold conversation about having a few songs by an artist does not mean that the person is a huge fan or even a fan at all. It is okay to have many interests. That sort of thing. A similar thing happened when she noticed that she thinks old photos of XXXXXXXXX look like XXXXXXXXX. (I don't particularly think so, but she does.) I've had to have very strong frank discussions about that after many repeated convos and questions.

She can remember specific details about events from years ago, that I can't even recall.

A OK

Q30 - OPTIONAL QUESTION The person with the Disorder of the Corpus Callosum Disorder: (You may choose more than one.)

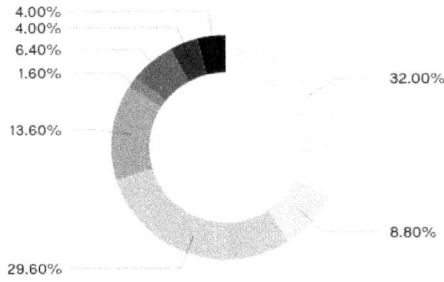

4.00%
4.00%
6.40%
1.60%
32.00%
13.60%
8.80%
29.60%

(ACC) Agenesis of the corpus callosum: All or a portion of the corpus callosum is absent; this includes both complete and partial ACC

(AgCC) Agenesis of the corpus callosum: All or a portion of the corpus callosum is absent. This acronym has appeared more recently in some research literature.

(c-ACC) Complete agenesis of the corpus callosum: The corpus callosum is completely absent.

(p-ACC) Partial agenesis of the corpus callosum: A portion of the corpus callosum is absent; most often it is the posterior (back) portion that is missing.

Hypogenesis of the corpus callosum: Another term sometimes used to describe partial ACC.

Hypoplasia of the corpus callosum: The corpus callosum is present, but is abnormally thin.

Dysgenesis of the corpus callosum: The corpus callosum is present but is malformed in some way; this includes p-ACC and Hypoplasia.

Unknown or Other

#	Answer	%	Count
1	(ACC) Agenesis of the corpus callosum: All or a portion of the corpus callosum is absent; this includes both complete and partial ACC	32.00%	40
2	(AgCC) Agenesis of the corpus callosum: All or a portion of the corpus callosum is absent. This acronym has appeared more recently in some research literature.	8.80%	11
3	(c-ACC) Complete agenesis of the corpus callosum: The corpus callosum is completely absent.	29.60%	37
4	(p-ACC) Partial agenesis of the corpus callosum: A portion of the corpus callosum is absent; most often it is the posterior (back) portion that is missing.	13.60%	17
5	Hypogenesis of the corpus callosum: Another term sometimes used to describe partial ACC.	1.60%	2
6	Hypoplasia of the corpus callosum: The corpus callosum is present, but is abnormally thin.	6.40%	8
7	Dysgenesis of the corpus callosum: The corpus callosum is present but is malformed in some way; this includes p-ACC and Hypoplasia.	4.00%	5
8	Unknown or Other	4.00%	5
	Total		125

Unknown or Other Responses

Unknown or Other - Text

My daughter has P-ACC and the anterior is absent

CT scan was not able to accurately determine partial or complete

She has partial ACC, but is missing some of the anterior portion, due to septopreoptic holoprosencephaly

Ventriculogmegaly of 1-3 as well.

Q31 - OPTIONAL QUESTION Does the person with DCC have other health or behavior concerns? Please list.

OPTIONAL QUESTION Does the person with DCC have other health or behavior concerns? Please list.

mental illness

Understanding social rules and regulations g emotions when upset

Bone delay (taking growth hormone) and chromosomal inversion on chromosome 13, no detentions or insertions - just inverted.

Eye issues, cognitive delays, leukemia (in remission), seizures,

No

Diabetes

Hearing loss, microcephaly

Cancer, Spine abifia,

anxiety,depression.

Anixody and depression

Hydrocephalus

hydrocephalus, colpocephaly, neurogenic spastic bladder, growth hormone deficiency, seizure disorder, stress induced adrenal insufficiency

ADHD, Epilepsy, chromosomal gain

Dsylexic

Seizures, Mental Retardation, Rheumatoid Arthritis, Bi-Polar, Migraines, Scoliosis, Bilateral Bunions
Delayed with all motor skills: fine motor, gross motor and motor planning.

ADHD and growth hormone disorder and hypermobility

Chiari malformation

Can't budget or hold down a job. Can't multitask. Can't stay organized. Vision problems and spasticity.

overweight

She has unbalanced Chromosome abnormality of 22p and 14Q, small degree of cerebral palsy, autistic tendencies, sensory issues, epilepsy with partial complex Seizures, periventricular leukomalacia, global developmental delays,

No

None

Autistic, registered blind.

Arnold chiari- acquired hydrocephalus seizures scoliosis Bangalore nerve stimulator

Anxiety/ADHD

borderline personality disorder, anxiety, morbid obesity, narcolepsy, cataplexy, pcos, depression
Just diagnosed at 79, acoustic neuroma, fluid on the brain
He also has cerrebeller vermis hypoplasia and a lipoma of the corpus Callosum.. We have issue with moods he misinterpretes tone wrong and will get very moody

because he thinks we used to weigh him. He also gets physically tired and that affects his mental ability to cope with things

Poor reaction time but not life threatening

Osteoarthritis orthopedic issues, depression, insomnia, high blood pressure, anxiety, factor V Leiden(blood disorder), high pain tolerance

Allergies and dyslexia speech impediment

Emotional regulation, anxiety, hydrocephalus, Schiari malformation

Cerebral palsy mild left extremeties

anxiety, depression, and some social issues

seizures controlled with medication, difficulty swallowing (specifically pills),
Hydrocephalus, cerebral palsy, strabismus, vision dark spots, trouble with decisions in new situations, confusion with which town he is in/finding places without a gps, directions
Depression, social awkwardness, inability to initiate conversation, asthma, autistic tendencies
seizure disorder, premenstrual mood swings that are sometimes intense

ADD: NVLD: APD

Anxiety, Major Depressive Disorder, Anorexia, and although not diagnosed officially yet, conversations with her psychologist & psychiatrist have discussed traits of bipolar II disorder and/or borderline personality disorder. She also has a history of self-harm and suicidal ideation.

Congenital heart defect (aortic stenosis)

Austistic like tendenxies. Social issues. Inabilty to read facial wxpressions and inability to inderstand simple emtional concepts

No

gets upset when he cant express himself, gets upset if other family members are upset

blood abnormality : deficit in factor 10

low muscle tone in left hand and side of body

Seizure disorder caused by ACC, and excessive/heterotophic grey matter on the right lateral ventricle

No

Scoliosis, eye problems, probable Kallmann syndrome (including anosmia), short stature, septopreoptic holoprosencephaly

non social, slow processing

non-verbal LD, hearing loss, low executive functioning, tetralogy of fallot, pancreaic divisum, torticollis, ptsd, deppression, anxiety, gets very emotional when trying to ask for help but not getting throughnto person. can become angry.

Social behavior issues.

Depression and anxiety; celiac disease

Colpocephaly, slight heart murmur

Panhypituitarism, Chiari One Malformatiom, hearing impaired

Diabetes type 2 high cholesterol , hypertension

Anger

OCD. depression. Learning disabilities. Mental health issues dealing with anger and rage. Unable to hold a job

hydrocephalus and Gorlin Syndrome and ADHD

CANCER SPINA BIFIDA

Hydrocephalus, Epilepsy, Chiari Malformation , DXed Autism

What is the prevalence of confabulation within the community of individuals with DCC? Keeping in mind that the purpose of this study was not to measure how extensively or how often persons with DCC confabulate but, rather, the percentage of people with DCC who confabulate; the answers of always, often, sometimes, and rarely are seen collaboratively as a positive response to this question. The data collected via this survey questionnaire is a measure of spontaneous confabulation, memory, or orientation forms of confabulation, not of provoked confabulation.

Of the 139 respondents, a total of 98 (70.5%) positively affirmed some incidents of spontaneous confabulation. Forty-one individuals (29.5%) responded "never." Of the responses considered positive for spontaneous confabulation, 31 (22.3%) indicated "rarely," an additional 45 (32.37%) responded "sometimes," 17 (12.23%) responded "often," with 5 (3.6%) indicating "(almost) always".

Reported Rate of Confabulation

Confabulation can be defined as communicating information that is untrue while perceiving that it is true. Does the person with the Disorder of the Corpus Callosum (DCC) confabulate spontaneously (on their own without prompting)?

Response	% of Respondents	Count
Never	29.5	41
Rarely	22.3	31
Sometimes	32.37	45
Often	12.23	17
(almost) Always	3.6	5

Does age affect rates of confabulation within the population with DCC? A cross tab of the 139 responses on age groups and affirmation or negation of reports of confabulation was positive for reports of confabulation across all age levels. There were 52 total responses reporting on persons under the age of 14, 14 ages 14-17, 14 ages 18-20, 19 ages 21-25, 14 ages 26-30, 6 ages 31-35, 9 ages 36- 40, 4 ages 41-45, and 6 ages 46 and older. In all age categories, more respondents rated individuals with DCC as confabulating than not. There was a chi-square value of 3.67, with 9 degrees of freedom, and a p-value of 0.93.

Age of Individual with DCC x Reported Rate of Confabulation

Age of individual with DCC	Total number of individuals	Total number of individuals answering "never confabulates"	% of individuals answering "never confabulates"	Total number individuals answering "sometimes, often, or (almost) always confabulates"	% of individuals answering "sometimes, often, or (almost) always confabulates"
Under 14	52	19	36.54	33	63.46
14-17	14	3	21.43	11	78.57
18-20	14	3	21.43	11	78.57
21-25	19	5	26.32	14	73.68
26-30	14	5	35.71	9	64.29
31-35	6	2	33.33	4	66.67
36-40	9	2	22.22	7	77.78
41-45	4	1	25.0	3	75.0
46+	6	1	16.67	5	83.33
Unknown	1	0	0.0	1	100.0

Does gender affect rates of confabulation within the population with DCC? There was a total of 97 responses to gender, with a total of 41 reports on males and 56 on females. A percentage of 17.07 of the reports on males responded "never," and 82.93% of the reports on males responded positive for incidences of confabulation. Of the reports on females, 19.64% responded "never," with 80.36% responding positive for incidences of confabulation. There was a chi-square value of 0.10, with 2 degrees of freedom, and a p-value of 0.95.

Gender of Individual with DCC x Confabulation Rate

	Never	% Never	Rarely, Sometimes, Often, (almost) Always	% Rarely, Sometimes, Often, (almost) Always	Total	% Total
Male	7	17.07	34	82.93	41	100.00
Female	11	19.64	45	80.36	56	100.00
Other	0	0.00	0	0.00	0	100.00
Total	18	18.56	79	81.44	97	100.00

Is there a discrepancy between self-reporting of confabulation and incident reporting by others? Of the 139 respondents, 34 were self-reporting and 106 were persons associated with and reporting on an individual with DCC. Of the self-reporting individuals, 32.35% said they "never" confabulate in opposition to the 28.3% of individuals associated with and individual with DCC who answered "never." Of note is the opposite end of the scale in which 2.94% of individuals with DCC self-reported "often" confabulating, and 15.09% of the persons associated with an individual with DCC reported "often." Similarly, 0.00% of individuals with DCC self-reported "(almost) always" confabulating and 4.72% of those individuals associated with an individual with DCC reported "(almost) always" confabulating (see Table 5). There was a chi-square value of 6.69, with 4 degrees of freedom, and a p-value of 0.15.

Spontaneous Confabulation in Individuals with DCC x

Self Reporting vs. Community Reporting

	Self Reporting	% Self Reporting	Community Reporting	% Community Reporting	Total	% Total
Never	11	32.35	30	28.30	41	29.50
Rarely	11	32.35	21	19.81	31	22.30
Sometimes	11	32.35	34	32.08	45	32.37
Often	1	2.94	16	15.09	17	12.23
(almost) Always	0	0	5	4.72	5	3.60
Totals	34	100	106	100	139	100

5 REFERENCES

Dalla Barba, G. (1993a). Confabulation: Knowledge and recollective experience. *Cognitive Neuropsychology*, *10*, 1-20. doi:10.1080/02643299308253454

Dalla Barba, G. (1993b). Different patterns of confabulation. *Cortex*, *226*, 525-534. doi:10.1016/s0010-9452(13)80281-x

Rensen, Y. C. M., Oosterman, J. M., van Damme, J. E., Griekspoor, S. I. A., Wester, A. J., Kopelman, M. D., & Kessels, R. P. C. (2015). Assessment of confabulation in patients with alcohol-related cognitive disorders: The Nijmegen–Venray confabulation list (NVCL-20). *The Clinical Neuropsychologist*, *29*, 804-823. doi:10.1080/13854046.2015.1084377

Roma, P., Sabatello, U., Verrastro, G., & Ferracuti, S. (2011). Comparison between Gudjonsson Suggestibility Scale 2 (GSS2) and Bonn Test of Statement Suggestibility (BTSS) in measuring children's interrogative suggestibility. *Personality and Individual Differences*, *51*, 488-491. doi:10.1016/j.paid.2011.05.003

Smith, E. A. (2011). *Confabulation and traumatic brain injury.* Berlin, Germany: LAP Lambert Academic Publishing.

Wright, Cheryl Lynn, "Confabulation in Individuals with Disorders of the Corpus Callosum: Educational Implications" (2017). *Dissertations.* Paper 133. https://digitalcommons.wku.edu/diss/133

ABOUT THE AUTHOR

Dr. Cheryl Wright is an advocate for individuals with disabilities. She enjoys being an international educator, speaker, and author. She has worked as a life-skills coach for students with developmental disabilities in South Korea, Thailand, Kuwait, and the United States. She is the author of the Cultural Rainbow series of children's books about individuals with different abilities, acceptance, holidays, and cultures around the world. She holds an advanced degree in Autism Spectrum Disorders and earned her Doctorate of Education from Western Kentucky University.

www.ingramcontent.com/pod-product-compliance
Lightning Source LLC
Chambersburg PA
CBHW070258290326
41930CB00041B/2640